Gratitude Journal

What a good day
to have a
Great Day

begin
each day
with a
grateful
heart

Hydration Station:

How many cups of water did you drink today?

Gratitude turns
what we have
into enough

- Henry Ward Beecher

Hydration Station:

How many cups of water did you drink today?

grat·i·tude

(noun): the quality of being thankful;
readiness to show appreciation for and
to return kindess.

TODAY'S
mindful
REFLECTIONS

Hydration Station:

How many cups of water did you drink today?

WHAT A PRIVILEGE IT IS

to be alive,
to think,
to enjoy,
to love.

- Marcus Aurelius

Hydration Station: 

How many cups of water did you drink today?

I

am
thakful
for today

Hydration Station:

How many cups of water did you drink today?

The more grateful I am,
the more beauty I see.

- Mary Davis

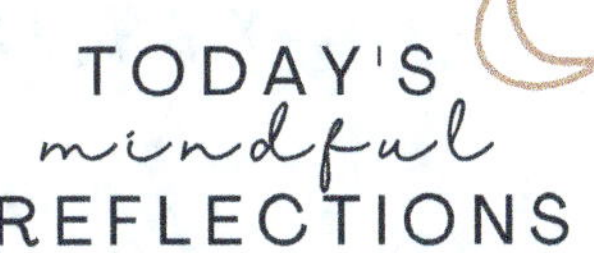

Hydration Station:

How many cups of water did you drink today?

Grateful for
small things,
big things,
and everything
in between

DATE: / /

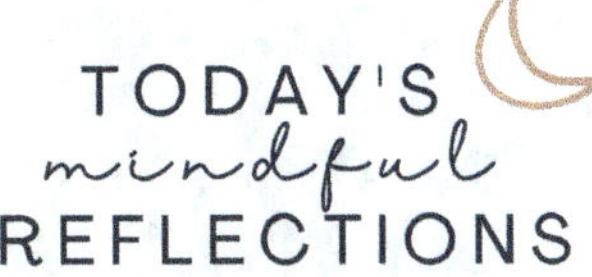

Hydration Station:

How many cups of water did you drink today?

You will never win
if you never begin

- Helen Rowland

Hydration Station: 

Be that kind
soul that
makes
everybody feel
like a
somebody

TODAY I'M *grateful* FOR

TODAY'S *feel good* GOALS

TODAY'S *mindful* REFLECTIONS

Hydration Station: 

How many cups of water did you drink today?

creating space by

getting rid of things that

no longer serve you

invites possibility,

opportunity, and

more space for love

- Miranda Anderson

Hydration Station: 

GRATITUDE +
GENEROSITY =
ABUNDANCE

Hydration Station:

GRATITUDE
OPENS
THE DOOR TO
THE POWER,
THE WISDOM,
THE CREATIVITY
OF THE
UNIVERSE

- DEEPAK CHOPRA

TODAY I'M
grateful
FOR

TODAY'S
feel good
GOALS

TODAY'S
mindful
REFLECTIONS

Hydration Station:

How many cups of water did you drink today?

Smile
laugh
& be
happy

TODAY I'M
grateful
FOR

TODAY'S
feel good
GOALS

TODAY'S
mindful
REFLECTIONS

Hydration Station: ⬯⬯⬯⬯⬯⬯⬯⬯⬯⬯

How many cups of water did you drink today?

Gratitude will shift
you to a higher
frequency,
and you will attract
much better things.

- Rhonda Byrne

Hydration Station: 〇〇〇〇〇〇〇〇〇〇

How many cups of water did you drink today?

GRATEFUL
FOR WHERE
I'M AT

EXCITED
FOR WHERE
I'M GOING

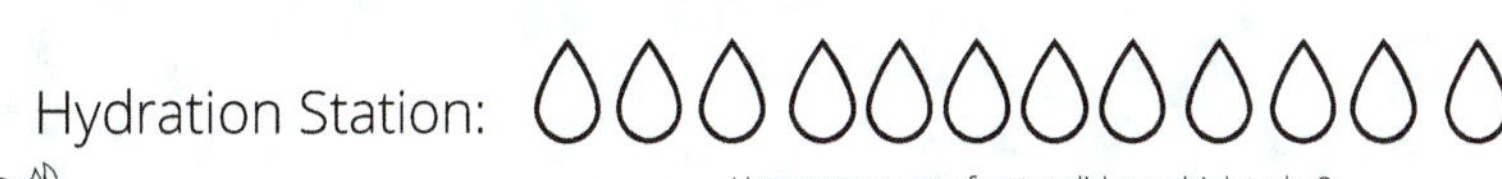

Hydration Station:

How many cups of water did you drink today?

As we express
our gratitude,
we must
never forget
that the highest
appreciate
is not
- John F. Kennedy .
to utter words,
but to live
by them

Hydration Station:

How many cups of water did you drink today?

Live every day
with the attitude
of gratitude

Hydration Station: ⬡⬡⬡⬡⬡⬡⬡⬡⬡⬡

How many cups of water did you drink today?

Showing gratitude
is one of the
simplest
yet most
powerful things
humans can do
for each other.

– Randy Pausch

TODAY'S
mindful
REFLECTIONS

Hydration Station: 

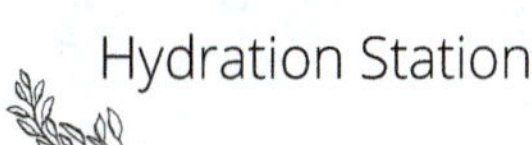

How many cups of water did you drink today?

Choose

Happy

Hydration Station:

Two kinds of gratitude:
The sudden kind we feel for
what we take; the larger kind
we feel for what we give.

- Edwin Arlington Robinson

DATE: /   /

TODAY I'M
grateful
FOR

TODAY'S
feel good
GOALS

TODAY'S
mindful
REFLECTIONS

Hydration Station:
How many cups of water did you drink today?

Beleive in yourself

TODAY'S
mindful
REFLECTIONS

Gratitude is a currency
that we can mint for
ourselves, and spend
without fear of
bankruptcy.

- Fred De Witt Van Amburgh

Hydration Station: 

How many cups of water did you drink today?

Be such a

beautiful soul

that people

crave your

vibes

Hydration Station: 

to speak gratitude is
courteous and
pleasant, to enact
gratitude is generous
and noble, but to live
gratitude is to touch
Heaven

- Johannes Gaertner

TODAY I'M
grateful
FOR

TODAY'S
feel good
GOALS

TODAY'S
mindful
REFLECTIONS

Hydration Station:

How many cups of water did you drink today?

be brave

be kind

be grateful

Hydration Station:

How many cups of water did you drink today?

ACKNOWLEDGING THE
GOOD THAT YOU
ALREADY HAVE IN
YOUR LIFE IS THE
FOUNDATION OF ALL
ABUNDANCE

- Eckhart Tolle

Hydration Station:

How many cups of water did you drink today?

MY *energy* IS MY POINT OF *attraction*

Hydration Station: 

Enjoy the little things,
for one day you may
look back and realize
they were the big
things

- Robert Brault

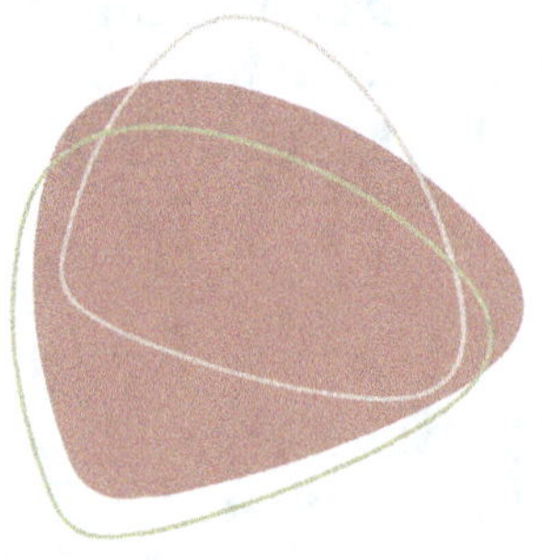

TODAY I'M
grateful
FOR

TODAY'S
feel good
GOALS

TODAY'S
mindful
REFLECTIONS

Hydration Station: ◌ ◌ ◌ ◌ ◌ ◌ ◌ ◌ ◌ ◌ ◌ ◌

How many cups of water did you drink today?

Start each day
with an attitude
of gratitude

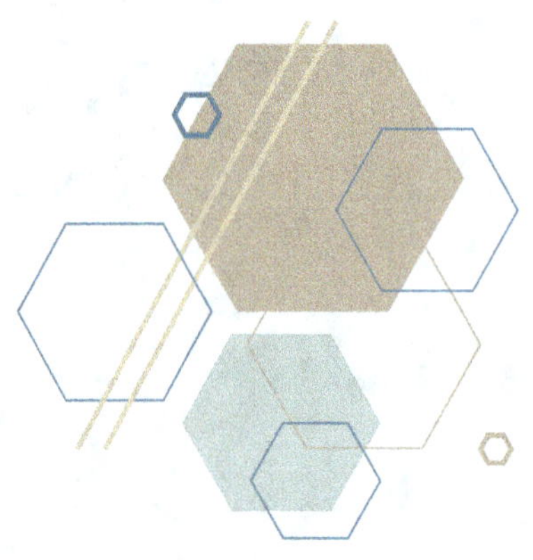

Hydration Station:

What a precious privilege
it is to be alive

to breathe, to think
to enjoy, to love

- Marcus Aurelius

TODAY'S
mindful
REFLECTIONS

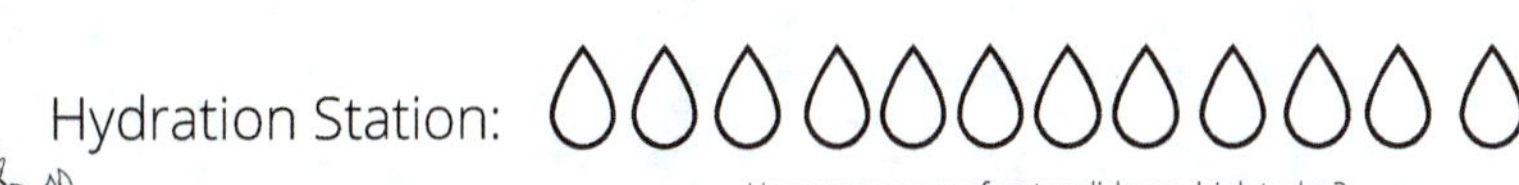

Hydration Station:

How many cups of water did you drink today?

Gratitude

helps you see

what's there

instead of

what isn't

Hydration Station:

How many cups of water did you drink today?

remember

that what you now have
was once among the things
you only hoped for

- Epicurus

Hydration Station:

How many cups of water did you drink today?

so grateful
for
so much

TODAY'S
mindful
REFLECTIONS

Hydration Station:

thank you.

MY NOTES

MY NOTES

MY NOTES

MY NOTES

www.ingramcontent.com/pod-product-compliance
Lightning Source LLC
Chambersburg PA
CBHW061518250726
48657CB00005B/1937